Master Woodturning: Beginner's Secrets to Success

Lucille .Q Tanner

All rights reserved. Copyright © 2023 Lucille .Q Tanner

Funny helpful tips:

Stay informed about the potential of digital IDs; they could redefine identity verification and security.

Rotate between different literary forms; poetry, prose, and drama each offer unique experiences and insights.

Master Woodturning: Beginner's Secrets to Success : Turn Your Hobby into a Profitable Skillset with Tips for Mastering Woodturning Techniques

__Life advices:__

Your spirit is a flame; keep it burning brightly, illuminating your path.

Cultivate a sense of wonder; it keeps the spirit young and vibrant.

Introduction

This is a comprehensive guide that provides valuable insights and practical knowledge for individuals looking to explore the art of woodturning. This guide covers a wide range of topics, from essential tools and safety measures to the intricate techniques of woodturning and project ideas.

At the outset, the guide introduces readers to the essential tools required for woodturning. It elaborates on specific tools like parting tools and offers advice on safety best practices, emphasizing the importance of personal protective equipment and maintaining a safe working environment.

The section on lathe components provides a thorough understanding of the lathe itself, including the headstock, tailstock, tool rest, and indexing wheel. Readers gain insights into the functionality of these components and how to make necessary adjustments.

Wood selection is a critical aspect of woodturning, and the guide delves into factors like durability, cost, tone, and ease of working with different types of wood. It also discusses the preparation of a log and the nuances of turning green wood bowls, explaining the challenges associated with cracking and offering insights into twice-turned projects.

Sharpening lathe tools is a skill every woodturner should master, and the guide covers this topic in detail. It explains the use of a grinder for sharpening woodturning tools, grinding angles, and various techniques to ensure tools are properly sharpened for precision work.

The guide explores specific woodturning techniques such as spindle turning, oval turning, and copy turning. It provides tips and guidelines for each technique, allowing beginners to experiment with different styles and shapes in their woodturning projects.

Project ideas are a significant part of this guide, with a focus on creating beautiful wooden bowls. It discusses the process of turning bowls, from marking out and tool preparation to shape turning and finishing touches. It even covers finishing techniques like sanding, polishing, and applying oil.

In summary, this book serves as a comprehensive and informative resource for those venturing into the world of woodturning. It equips beginners with knowledge about tools, safety, lathe components, wood selection, sharpening, and various woodturning techniques. With project ideas for bowls, this guide provides a solid foundation for individuals looking to embark on their woodturning journey.

Contents

Chapter One Tools 1

The Parting Tools 1

Safety 6

Safety Best Practices 8

The Environment 8

Health State 9

Personal Protective Equipment 9

Around the Lathe 11

The Faceplate Mounting 11

Speed of the Lathe 12

Adjusting 12

The Spur Chuck Mount 13

The Tailstock 13

The Tool Rest 13

The Hand Confirmation 13

In the End 14

Chapter Two 16

Size Variance 16

The Lathe Parts 16

The Headstock 17

Speed and Power Alternator 18

The Lathe Base 19

The Tool Rest 19

The Indexing Wheel 19

The Tailstock	20
Accessories	20
Chapter Three Lathe Maintenance	21
Maintenance ChecklistRust	21
Tailstock and Banjo	22
Dirt	22
The Belts	22
Tool Rest Check	23
Thread Checks	23
Chapter Four Selecting Wood	25
The Durability	25
Cost of Purchase	26
Tone and Hue	26
Ease of working with	26
Preparing a log	27
Chapter Five Turning Green Wood Bowls	31
Dry and Wet	31
Cracking	32
Twice Turned	35
Why Greenwood?	36
Chapter Six Sharpening Lathe Tools	37
The Grinder	38
Using a Grinder to Sharpen Woodturning Tools	39
Grinding Angles	40
Chapter SevenTechniques	42
Chatter	42
Spindle Turning Foundation	43

Oval Turning	46
The Turning of a Tenon on a 4-Jaw Chuck	47
Chapter Eight Copy turning	48
Copy turning attachment	48
Tips for copy turning	52
Marking Out	53
Tool Preparation	53
Shape Turning	54
Chapter Nine Finishing Sanding	55
Polishing papers and cloths	57
Oil application	59
Friction Polishing	60
Chapter Ten Projects Bowls	62
Fancy String Pulls	66
Weed Pots	69
Wood Bangles	75
Pen	79
Wooden Mug	83

Chapter One
Tools

The number of tools available on the market for woodturning is mind-boggling and deciding on which to buy and use as a beginner can cause some serious headaches. For starters, buy an all-around set with five tools that most times are used to get most projects done.

The woodturning art is similar to wood carving as it involves the calculated and gradual removal of wood in specified areas on a piece of wood to reveal the end product. To get this done, the crafter needs to have certain basic tools, which are generally divided into carbide-insert turning tools and the traditional turning tools.

The traditional tools are aptly named because they have been in use by woodworkers for ages. With the advent of new technologies, however, you have the choice to use tools made from high-grade steel that can work and withstand a lot of adverse environmental conditions. Some of these basic tools are familiar to many crafters who have had years of relationship with them. For beginners, however, who are still finding their feet, I will touch on the common traditional tools used in woodturning to get you familiarized with the tools of the trade.

The Parting Tools

These implements are constructed for use in shearing off a section of the completed section of a spindle from the stock's main body. Other than for the parting function for which they were mainly designed, these tools can also be used to cut grooves and other designs on the spindle. The cutting edges can either be circular-shaped, square-shaped, or any other shape that the woodworker might require.

The Skew Chisels

They are the perfect tools for constructing V-grooves; shearing cuts through the action of the sharp inclined edges. The inclined or angled cutting edge can be curved or straight. The chisels come in various forms, which can be used based on the woodworker's discretion and the project at hand. As with any new tool, you need patience and constant practice to get the hang of maximizing this tool's potentials best.

Gouges
The gouges can be divided into spindle gouges, bowl gouges, and roughing gouges. The bowl turning gouge is installed on the lathe so that it lays flush to the turning area. You will discover that the bowl gouge is typically worked on with indentations and straight-up surfaces to absorb the workload they are subjected to comfortably. The spindle gouge and roughing gouge, on the other hand, are employed in the turning of spindles. Here, the stock or blank is loaded on the machine so that the grain's flow faces the turning area directly. Spindle gouges are perfect for creating beads, coves, etc., while the roughing gouge is used to create round forms from square ones. The tools are created for particular jobs, and ideally, they shouldn't be used for jobs that they weren't created for. You should note that you should ever use a roughing gouge on a bowl stock on no account. It doesn't have the strength for this particular task, and there is the likelihood that the bowl will come loose during the process, and an accident and damage to the tool might occur.
Besides the above-described tools, you will also find highly specialized tools used to form dovetailed indents and bead shapes.
These tools need to be sharpened right on schedule; you can set up a logbook on when all your tools should undergo this process. You should have a slow speed grinder in your workshop to be used for the sharpening. Going about sharpening your tools manually might not produce the desired results as the tools have varied and have different requirements. With tools such as chisels, as stated earlier, practice is essential to make proper use of it, and with a method

termed "riding the bevel," you are guaranteed of getting an outcome you dream about.

"Riding the bevel" is a must-know method of turning for beginners as it ensures that you fully understand how to make use of the traditional turning tools. To begin with this technique, the implement should make firm touch with the tool rest. Then gradually push the tool till the bevel of the cutting area comes in contact with the turning stock. Kindly note that no cutting will be taking place yet. With this position in place, gently press the tool towards you and, at the same time, lift the lever of the tool, and the cutting surface will then start to turn the blank and shavings produced. With the turning in progress, ever so gently, move the tool into an inclination in flow with the cut.

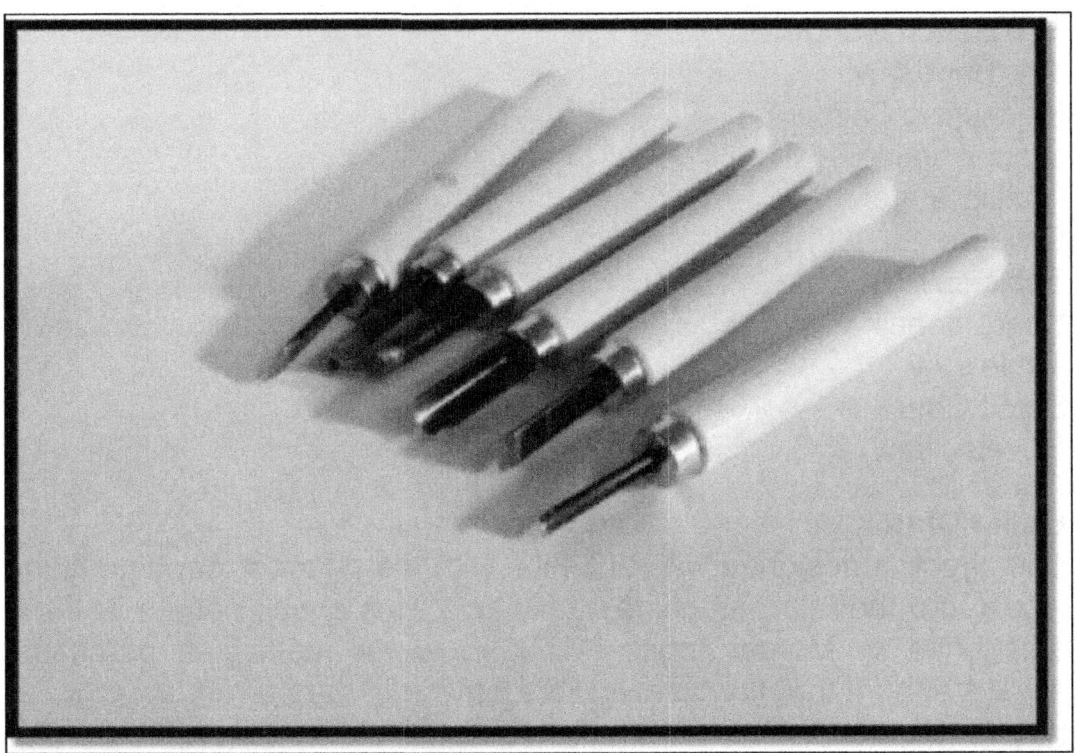

Also to be considered is whether you want tools made of high-speed steel or carbon steel. The high-speed steel tools are more expensive than carbon steel varieties. You also won't need to grind them as often as you would with the carbon steel tools because they hold the sharpened edge much longer. This result in having a tool that has a longer lifespan and devoid of such risks as the loss of hardness and bluing that is likely to occur with regular grinding. With experience, you will become more comfortable with a wider range of tools, and you can then begin to experiment with ones you feel will add value to your projects.

Additional tools
The Scraper

It also comes in various sizes and shapes, just like the chisels. You should, however, consider two or three as a good addition to your box.

The Bench Grinder
The Bandsaw
Measuring Calipers
Woodworking awl
A utility knife
Dividers
Table saw
Sharp pencil
Table saw
Scroll Chuck
Dovetail saw

Collet Chuck

The chuck is designed with drill bits, with the chuck's rear side fitting nicely into the lathe machine's tailstock. This chuck comes in three categories of Morse Taper (MT), so when making a purchase, always ensure that the size you are buying is the correct size for the lathe's tailstock.

Multi Jawed Chuck / Jaw Chuck
It is built specifically to grip and hold the wood in place on the lathe machine. There are screws on the chuck that can be controlled to increase or reduce the jaws' size. Just like with the Collet chuck, you also need to buy a Jaw chuck that is the correct size for the lathe.

Safety

When you consider that the lathe machine, the rotation of a blank, sharp and pointed machinery all moving at a fast pace, you will come to understand the absolute need for safety in these conditions. Protecting yourself is paramount, as well as any other person in the vicinity, and the integrity of your machine and other tools. Before we go into detailed points on safety requirements, I will quickly touch on a few basics of ensuring safety in the workspace.

The barest minimum safety requirements that should be in place before you begin woodturning are;

- A proper face shield covers all parts of your face, including your eyes, nose, mouth, chin, etc. No part of

your face must be left exposed for whatever reason.
- You must put on a Turner's apron at all times when you are turning to prevent wood dust and shavings from attaching to your clothes.
- A proper respirator must be worn to prevent wood dust inhalation that can result in severe respiratory problems.
- It is also advisable that you put on clothing that will prevent your skin from coming in contact with wood dust and shavings as these can most likely result in allergic skin irritations.
- Do not carry out woodturning with loose-fitting clothes, belt hanging from any part of our body, neck chain, or any form of jewelry, etc., as they can get caught in the lathe while turning.
- Ensure that the stock is secured properly in the lathe machine to cut out the probability of shaking when the machine is running.
- The stock been worked on should be run at the correct speed.
- The lathe should be installed at a height that reaches your elbow.
- The tool rest should not be far away from the stock so that there won't be situations of it been hinged between the project at hand and the tool rest.
- The tool rest should ideally be removed before any sanding can take place.
- Do not sand towards you; rather, the piece should be held in such a way that the spin faces in the opposite direction away from your body.

Safety Best Practices

Under this section, I will be discussing some pertinent wood practices that every woodturner, both beginners and experienced hands, must always put at the top of their list before the start of every project.

The months or years you have spent woodturning counts a lot as you will have learned things to avoid and things to do to ensure every project's successful outcome. When an issue occurs that dumfounds you, you should take time to find out the cause and rectify it. This will ensure that such issues do not come up again, and you have added a skill set to your repertoire.

The Environment

When it comes to woodturning, your surroundings are a critical aspect of the practice that cannot be overlooked when it comes to your well-being and others around you. Where the lathe machine is installed should not be clogged with any form of materials, tools, or any object that can impede free movement. There will always be the presence of power cords around the machine, and the danger that they can cause cannot be underestimated, so make sure that the power cords are kept on the rear side of the lathe machine out of direct contact with you.

The moment you set your blank to the lathe, shavings immediately begin to appear, and the build-up on the floor is rapid. You might decide to allow the shavings to build up on the floor to provide some form of cushion for your legs and to act as a buffer when any of your tools fall to the floor. The presence of shavings on the floor works for some folks and doesn't for others. A large amount of shavings can make it hard to locate small pieces of tools that fall into it, and it can also lead to falls when the floor is not designed to have such materials on it. You can get a piece of soft and large rug to provide some sort of comfort for your legs. The rug will also capture a large amount of shavings that you can easily move out and dispose of properly. The shavings are not the only byproduct of the turning process; there will also be wood dust that can get into your lungs. You can mitigate this material's presence by installing dust filters and putting on a recommended air respirator at all times.

Health State

In as much as the state of the machine and the environment is important, nothing trumps the state of the human that will be operating the lathe. The human body will always have its off days, and at such times, the wise course of action to take is to take a break and come back to the lathe machine when you feel much better. Any health state other than a fully fit, painless, and attentive person can bring about severe physical injuries. Immediately you begin to notice yourself making errors that you will normally not make, or slight tiredness, switch off the machine and walk away. Take care of yourself, and when you are feeling much better with all your faculties in top shape, you can then return to turning.

Personal Protective Equipment

Whenever you step into the workspace to get some work done, you should, as a point of caution, put on all your protective gear even when the machine hasn't been switched on yet. Switch on the air filter system, put on your air respirator, face shield, proper clothing, and you can then proceed with turning.

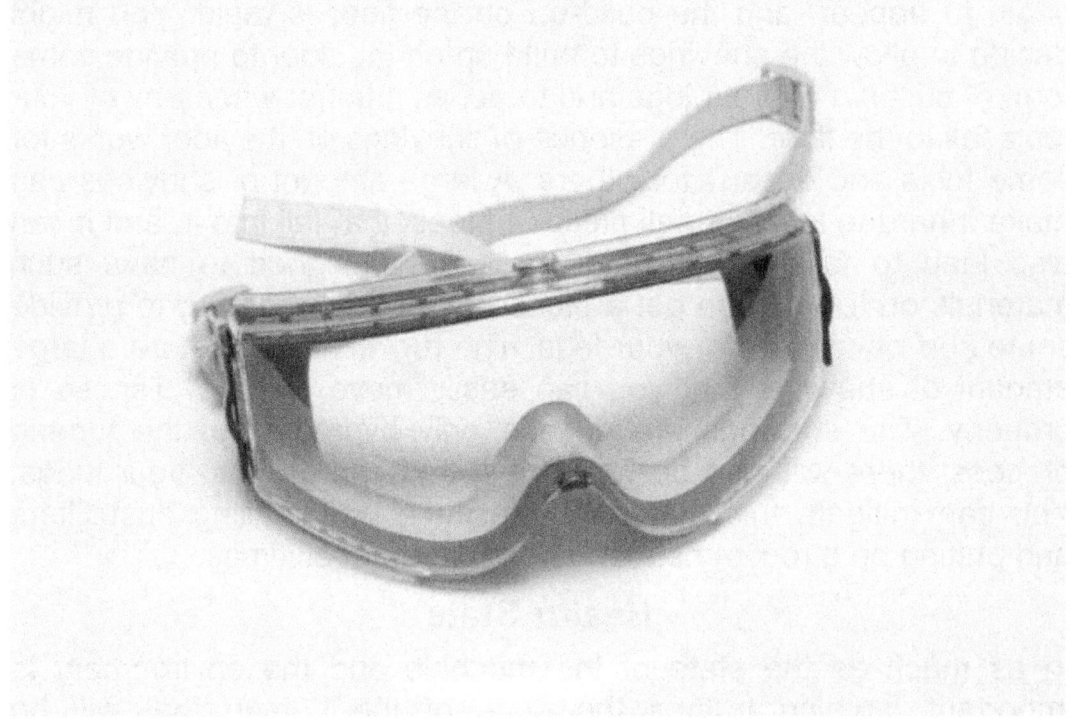

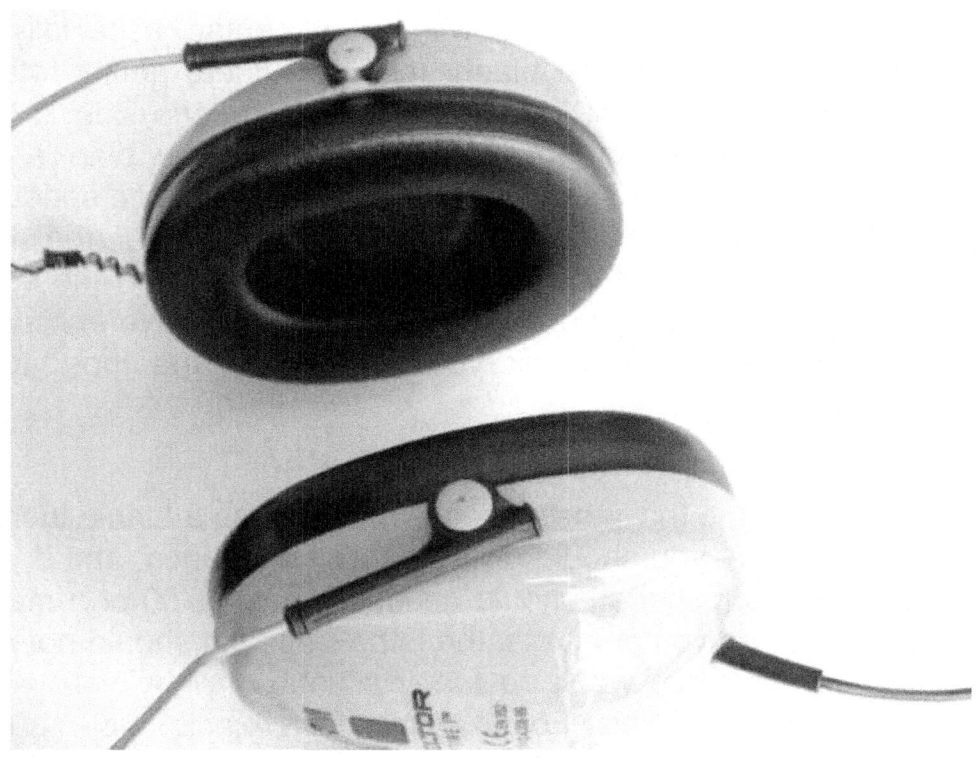

Around the Lathe

When you are ready to begin with the turning, ensure there are no tools or materials around the lathe. Check for any objects lying close or on the lathe and remove them. Before putting on the machine, check that it is at the lowest possible speed and then gradually increase it as you continue turning.

The Faceplate Mounting

With faceplate mounting, the go-to screws are the wood screws. Any other type of screw can fail at the most important of times. Set the screws to properly hold on the blank so that it will not distort the project's design at hand. The screws should also be resting totally on the surface of the faceplate. Ensure that the blank's rear side rests comfortably on the headstock with none of the spindle threads showing. If the faceplate is not resting comfortably on the headstock spindle shoulder, the turning will be off-center, especially when turning a bowl. When the blank has been fitted, gently rotate the blank manually to check if it tilts more towards one side. If the off-centered orientation cannot be altered due to the blank's shape, then the turning will have to be carried out at a reduced speed. If, on the other hand, the blank is balanced with no off-center, the speed is gradually increased till vibrations begin to occur, then the speed is reduced to achieve a smooth turning. When you have achieved the desired shape from the blank, you can increase the speed to clean up the cut.

Speed of the Lathe

When it comes to the lathe's speed when turning a blank, there is no fixed speed, but you should go with your experience, and if you are a beginner, your speeds should be ideally below 700 or a maximum of 800 r.p.m. As you progress, the lathe's speeds should not exceed 1000 r.p.m as there won't be many situations when you will need speeds higher than this. For example, for projects such as spindle turning, however, due to the relatively smaller area compared to bowls, for example, need a higher speed to cover the outer area of the wood. A three-inch diameter spindle blank been worked on with a 1000 r.p.m. is moving at a slower rate than a fifteen-inch bowl blank at the same speed. In other to counter this rate of speed for turning spindles generally are higher when compared to bowls.

Adjusting

When the lathe is rotating, and you need to make any slight change or correction to the tool rest, always make sure that the lathe is stopped. This may seem a bit tad inconvenient, but it is better that it is done than to have an accident happen. The constant correction of the tool rest for it to attain a stance to give you easy and unencumbered access should be taken seriously while also considering your safety.

The Spur Chuck Mount

The spur chuck must be properly driven into the blank before it is placed on the lathe. You should use a soft mallet, preferably one made of rubber, to drive it to avoid the disfiguring of the project. With the pair of the spur chuck and blank mounted on the headstock, shift the tailstock into position and secure it adequately onto the lathe. Check how tight the tailstock is during the turning process, as it will come slightly undone during the process.

The Tailstock

The combination of the tailstock, four-jaw chuck mount, or the faceplate will always provide extra stability when a bowl blank is loaded. If the project at hand is off-centered or not equally distributed, this arrangement will give you all the stability needed. Avoid employing a dead center with a tailstock as it results in scorching and quick deterioration of areas around where the contact is made.

The Tool Rest

All the lathe tools have different functions, and they all need slight altering when a blank is loaded. So for the tool rest, you need to make slight changes for all tools. You will get accustomed to this with plenty of hours of experience under your belt. When you load a blank and begin to turn, shavings are removed. The bowl blank will inevitably start to lose mass and gradually shift away from the tool rest and you. This will lead to the bowl's instability, leading to some pretty wild vibrations, which can be hazardous if it's not quickly stopped and adjusted.

The Hand Confirmation

With the stock properly secured on the mount, set the tool rest and the banjo into their correct positions. Move the headstock hand control and check it to ensure that the blank is not moving and will not make any form of contact with any area of the lathe machine once the turning process begins.

The Finish
When sanding with the lathe, make sure you are putting on your full protective gear, especially your respirator. Shift all the moving parts of the lathe away from the blank to avoid any obstruction. In applying finishes such as varnish and oil, it is imperative that the machine must not be in motion. It is a highly dangerous affair to use a piece of clothing to apply the finish while the machine is still rotating. Just as I discussed earlier, no loose material in whatever form should come close to the machine while it is rotating. Rather than making use of clothing, you can use a piece of solid foam that has no thread that can get caught in the rotating machine.

In the End

When you are through with the turning, carry out a proper cleaning of the surroundings, put all the tools in their proper places. Materials that are no longer needed should be discarded strictly following the directions on the packs.

If you have to constantly move heavy pieces of logs or other equipment within the workspace, you should use a trolley as the unwarranted lifting result in muscle strains. You can also break the loads into smaller parts if it is possible. It goes without saying that the floor should be clear of all forms of debris that can trip you while moving stuff around the room. Heavy objects can also fall either from the lathe or bench top, causing serious injuries to the body parts, especially your foot. A proper workspace boot fully equipped with steel toecaps will go a long way in giving you some measure of protection.

There is a rare chance of an electrical accident happening if the circuit is not properly grounded or some naked wiring is in direct contact with the lathe. The current flow is aided if there is water on the floor, and you are standing directly on it while working. The current will flow straight through your body, causing severe damage or even death. A regular check of all electrical connections is to be carried out, and install an earth leakage apparatus that will break the circuit if there is ever an electrical fault. Avoid moisture in whatever form in the workspace. Don't under any guise make use of faulty electrical gadgets even as a stop-gap measure until you can get high quality and recommended devices.

In addition to a wet floor been able to cause electrical injuries or death, it could also be responsible for falls. All the areas within the workspace should be dry at all times and constantly check for the presence of water, oils, or any other form of fluids that might have dripped or spilled to the floor. They become an increased source of danger. Always remove ropes, wirings, or any other form of loose materials lying on the floor as they can trip you. If there are uneven slopes, temporary platforms, or holes within the environment, make sure that you pay prompt attention to such situations before it deteriorates and becomes a source of potential danger to everyone around.

The danger of fire is real, and it can be ignited from electrical faults, steel wools catching fires from sparks produced from the lathe. Other combustible materials such as shavings, oily rags, dust, etc., can easily come alight from heat sources such as a bulb, spark, or embers from a cigarette butt. Make use of LED bulbs as they generate little to no heat, dispose of oil rags as recommended, sweep all shavings from the floor after each turning session, and not smoke in your workspace. If you must smoke, take a break, go outside some distance away from the workspace to enjoy your break.

With woodturning, safety is paramount, and carrying out all of these steps regularly becomes a habit that you imbibe and practice in your workspace in your drive towards producing amazing turned woodworks all the time.

Chapter Two
Buying a lathe and accessories

With your interest in woodturning heightened and the urge to get started and buying a lathe always there, it is pertinent that you are conversant with the parts of the machine, more so if you are a beginner. You will most likely not be too sure which part is which or what its functions are. This chapter will discuss the foundation of the lathe and guide you in identifying the parts of the machines and other important accessories.

Size Variance

The lathes' sizes vary, and the names are based on how large they are relative to each other. The most common type of lathes are the biggest ones that you will most likely find in many workshops. They do not require to be placed on a bench or any other form of support as they are constructed to support their weight. Going down, we have the medium-sized lathes that are in between the large and mini lathes. They are mostly not free-standing and can be placed on a bench or other forms of support. The smallest type of lathes are the mini-lathes, and they are structured for handling small woodturning projects. You will not find them been used to turning bowl blanks or other large projects; rather, they are good for projects such as pen turning. These are the major classification of lathes available even though there are other labels available. The larger varieties of lathes are distinguished by the inclusion of numbers to the name. The numbers added indicate the swing diameter and the lathe's bed length, e.g., 1236. Notwithstanding the lathe's size, they all have the same basic structure, parts, and functionalities.

The Lathe Parts

The lathe's identification will always be from the point of reference known as the working side of the machine. This is the lathe area that the woodworker operates the machine from; although there are

other sides, they do not give as much free room and ease of operation as the working side does. This doesn't mean that situations will arise when you have to take a stance on the opposite side; the times just rarely occur, and the majority of your work is mostly carried out in front of the machine, which is the work side.
Standing in front of the lathe, the drive mechanism and the motor referred to as the machine's headstock will be to your left-hand side.

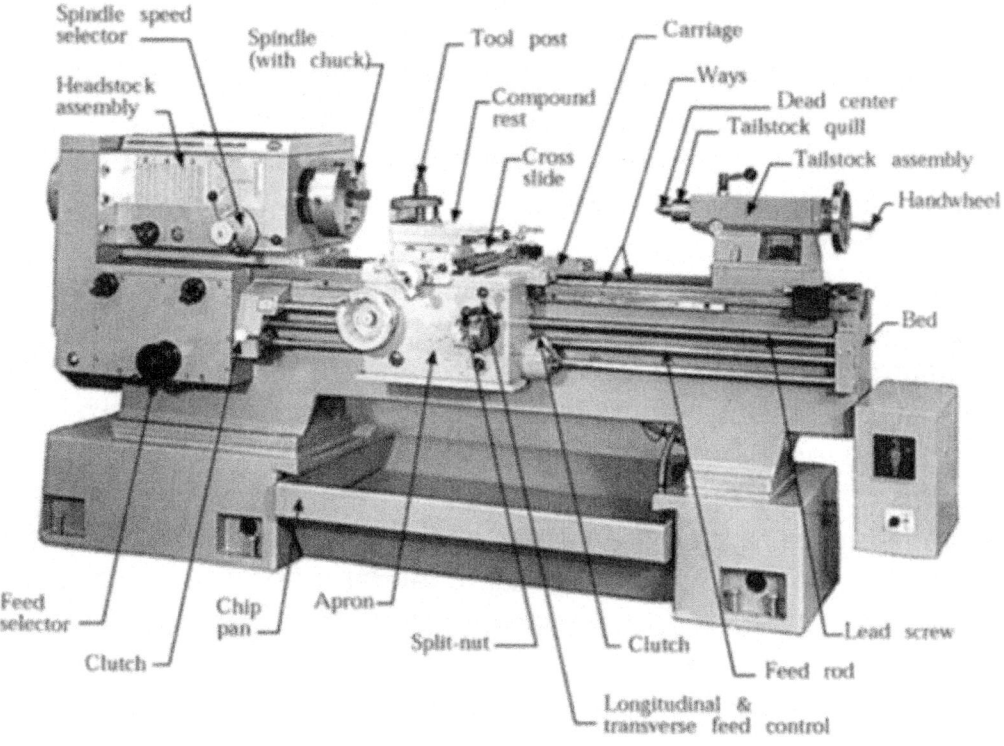

The Headstock

This is where all the activities of woodturning on a lathe starts. The drive belt, tension pulleys, and motor are situated here. The number and arrangement of the pulleys vary according to the type of lathe. The pulley gives control over the alteration of the speed of the machine by the user. Closely attached to this is a tension lever that serves to elevate the motor's position, bringing about a reduction of the tension on the drive belt and resulting in ease of change to another tension pulley. Before buying a lathe machine, check if it comes with a chart or instruction on the drive belt. Lathes that do not have multiple belts do not require that the user make constant adjustments to alter the machine's speed.

At the rear side of the headstock is the headstock spindle, which you will notice is threaded. This piece is often differentiated by the presence of threads, which are in varying sizes and numbers. A typical head spindle has a thread per inch (TPI) count of about 12. Another important feature is the Morse Taper, an indentation on the headstock spindle to secure any additional tool. Knowing the size of Morse Taper on your lathe will guide you when buying accessory tools to be used.

The lathe bed is comprised of a dual set of rails that set the length of the machine.

The distance between the top of the bed and the headstock center is called the lathe swing, which is an important factor in the size of a blank that the machine can work on.

To the left of the headstock is the hand wheel that comes into play when you want to reduce the lathe's speed after a turning session or to hasten the stopping of its rotation. It is also used to confirm if the tool rest won't obstruct the blank. The hand wheel is to be used at all times when you want to slow down the lathe.

Speed and Power Alternator

The speed button's position is not to be found in the same location on all lathe machines. You will find the switch at arms reach on your lathe working side in some brands to enable you to have absolute control over the machine's speed and power at all times. This cuts down on the need for you to walk a distance to power off or adjust the speed. The speed control mechanism is often in the form of a dial with speed variance showing on it. On some other models, the indicator is shown on an LED screen.

The Lathe Base

The foundation of any lathe machine is what confers actual solidity to the whole process. It does not matter the size or nature of wood been turned; a stable base is essential for the lathe and will affect the project's eventual outcome. For large free-standing lathes, they need to be standing on a solid floor, and the base should be strong enough to withstand high r.p.m without vibrating too much to disrupt the turning. On the other hand, if the lathe is sitting on a bench or other support forums, the table must have enough stability to prevent vibration when the blank is not naturally centered.

The Tool Rest

On the right side of the lathe is the tool rest support system, which is also called the banjo or the carriage. The banjo has its securing mechanism used to fix it in place at any location on the lathe bed, and the same applies to the tool rest.

The Indexing Wheel

You will mostly find the indexing wheel located around the headstock region of the lathe. It is a tool designed to help a woodworker determine the angle of rotation of the blank. The indexing wheel's general design comprises marks with numbers, while some do not have any form of markings at all. After determining and marking the blank center, release the pin before turning to avoid damages to the lathe. You will also notice the headstock spindle lock used in securing the spindle when accessories and other stuff are to be taken off the machine. The indexing wheel can be easily confused for the headstock spindle lock. No matter the type of lock used, always make sure that it is properly released and freed before you begin to run the machine.

The Tailstock

The tailstock is found on the right side of the lathe, and it is secured to the bed rails with the ability of easy mobility along the machine's length. The quill/live center is situated on the upper left side of the tailstock. This is designed to contain other essential tools that may be used for turning. The spindle lock of the tailstock secures the tailstock.

Accessories

These are tools that are optional when purchasing the lathe. You can always get to buy them separately. Examples include and are not limited to; drive center and live, wood lathe faceplate, center for the tailstock, bar wrenches for adjustment points, four-jaw chuck, knockout bar, specialty tools, extra tool rest, curved tool rest, etc.

Chapter Three
Lathe Maintenance

Just like with any other woodworking equipment, the lathe must be put on a regular maintenance schedule. Do not overlook this habit-forming with your lathe, as it will go a long way in ensuring that your machine continues to function seamlessly for a long time. With constant use, the lathe will accumulate a lot of dirt, dust, and other unwanted materials that will most likely hinder the lathe's smooth running. You should not wait until the machine begins to show signs of disuse and not turning as it should. You should draw up a maintenance schedule based on how often the machine is used. Every 40 to 50 days is an ideal time frame for you to tune the lathe.

Maintenance Checklist
Rust

You will sometimes have to turn blanks that have high moisture content, such as greenwood. Though it's an enjoyable experience for you, your lathe may suffer if appropriate actions are not promptly taken after the turning. The moisture from the wood covers the surface of the wood and encourages the formation of rust. Different types of woods have varied effects on metallic surfaces due to the type of compounds they have and the moisture.

If you notice the formation of rust on the lathe, you can spray a rust cleaning agent on the areas that need to have rust removed from. Sometimes the rust won't go away as quickly as it should or continues to work its damage. In situations like this, get a piece of sandpaper and sand thoroughly the areas that need attention. After the sanding, spray the rust cleaning or treatment agent before using a ball of fine steel wool to smoothen the area again gently. With this, the probability of rust forming in that area is greatly reduced.

Kindly note that the sandpaper used for the oxidation removal shouldn't be used on your wooden projects.

Tailstock and Banjo

Detach these parts from the lathe and gently methodically clean out accumulated dirt in whatever form from the surface, nooks, and crannies. After the cleaning is done, apply the appropriate type of lubricating oil to all the areas in constant touch with the machine's bedrails. Make sure that lubricating oil is applied to all moving parts of the banjo and tailstock. Take care not to over-apply the lubricant as this can lead to problems of its own. With the cleaning and lubrication done, these parts will slide easily over the bedrails, and all the parts will also lock and unlock with ease.

The bed rails should also be lubricated regularly before it becomes a problem for it to move as it should. Before the application of the lubricant, make sure that it is cleaned and then dried. Proceed to apply the recommended paste wax, allow it dry then rub down with a piece of clean cloth.

Dirt

The accumulation of dust is the most common form of problem when it comes to the lathe's proper functioning. Shavings and dust can be cleaned up easily after each turning session; however, you have to carry out a proper clean up of the machine as dusting won't do a proper job. For this, get a vacuum cleaner to get to those hard to reach areas. The vacuum or compressor should be used to force out dust and dirt from crevices. Regular sweeping of shavings should also be a practice carried out after turning.

The Belts

The connecting belt between the headstock and the motor requires regular checkups too. Switch off the machine and disconnect it from the power mains, unscrew any protective coverings that might be housing the belts. Manually move the belt and check every area for fraying or any other damages. If the belt has begun to lose its integrity, kindly make a change immediately. Every area around the belt area should also be checked for any build-up of dirt that needs to be removed.

Tool Rest Check

The tool rest will inevitably suffer from damage through use, and you will become aware of this when there is a sudden catch and smashing of a gouge or scraper against the tool rest. These obstructions to the flow of work of the tool rest will hinder its use by other tools. The tool rest will have ugly markings and nicks on its topmost parts, which is an indication for urgent attention. To fix this, use a file to form straight inclined strokes on the affected areas to get rid of the gouges. If you are purchasing a lathe for the first time, go for a machine with a tool rest made of premium steel because it is not subjected to such damage when compared to one made out of cast iron.

Thread Checks

Cross threading is a common problem with the headstock spindle, resulting in problems when trying to fix the faceplate or chuck. It also results in friction, and the fixing of any other tool with threads can be a headache.

When you notice that the faceplate or any other tool is hard to thread, check for where the problem is coming from and attempt at threading a different tool to confirm if the problem will persist. On checking with other tools and the threading won't still go easily points to the headstock thread been faulty. Assuming that it was just one tool that wasn't threading easily will point to the fact that it was that tool having the issue and not the headstock spindle itself.

To solve the threading problem:

> 1. Get a small brush or toothbrush, clean the grooves in the tool and the headstock spindle, and thread it again. If the problem persists, spray on some lubricating oil and try to thread it again.

2. If none of these methods are working, take a detailed look at the headstock spindle's threads.
3. Check the valleys and the ridges for grooves, scratches, and cuts; use a tiny metal file to gently file the area of interest.

With this done, you should have no problem with threading any tool to the headstock. If you are still encountering obstacles in threading, then a die that is the correct match for the headstock spindle is the final solution. Place the die on the headstock and gently rotate it until it can easily move up and down the headstock spindle. That will surely get the problem sorted out.

Threading of accessory tools that have been cross-threaded can be done using a brass bristle to brush it. Another way to handle it is by using a tap with the same measurement as the headstock spindle. Apply a bit of lubricant to the area before you tap it.

It goes without saying that a well-maintained lathe will continuously give you joy while turning with no problems. Pay close attention to the state of your machine, and you won't have to pay for the damages and costs that will most definitely result from a faulty piece of equipment.

Chapter Four
Selecting Wood

With woodturning, you have the choice of picking any type of tree and using almost any part of it for your project. The issue is that you will find that specific parts of the tree are better candidates for turning particular types of projects. There is also the issue of stability. This means the tendency for wood to move or warp during turning or dehydration. The more stable the wood is, the less likely it is to move or warp during any of the processes named earlier. A stable wood is a good choice for turning.

You are probably just picking up interest in turning, or you have some experience and need a guide on picking a wood type for a project at hand. I will be honest with you, selecting wood from the hundreds of species available can be a herculean task. This chapter will provide you with concise points to help you along with your task.

The Durability

A point to note, how hard a wood is not the same as the grouping of the tree as a hardwood. Hardwoods have to do with the scientific grouping of trees based on the type of seeds. For example, some softwoods are classified as hardwoods. Taking a close look at the durability of a tree, certain features are closely related to it, such as insect resistance, rot resistance, and density, also referred to as hardness.

A tree's ability to survive and thrive in the presence of attacks from insects and moisture varies; thus, some woods are better used for projects in very moist environments as they have the resistance to do well there. Though there is no harm in applying some level of protection to the wood in whatever environment you decide to use, it is always better to select a naturally resistant wood to harmful environmental conditions.

The higher the density of wood, the harder the wood is. These factors are not equal to each other, and hardwood will require extra work to get the desired result. Dense woods used for wooden projects confers sufficient heft and weight to the work. This quality also makes the product more appreciated depending on its end-use. Hardwoods are more resistant to mechanical wear and tear that they will most likely undergo in their everyday use.

Cost of Purchase

This is a point that is staring at you right in the face, yet most folks will assume it to be of no importance. To get the best idea on the price of wood required for our woodworking project, check around your local hardware stores, and if they don't carry your choice of wood, you can go online. There are many wood sellers online that deal in a wide variety of specialty wood with prices attached. You should know how much it will cost you to get the size and type of wood you need to keep cost in check, especially if you are working on a commissioned project.

Tone and Hue

Coloring and staining of wood are ways of bringing out the beauty and increasing the project's value. There are several ways to increase the hue or tone of the wood, e.g., ebonizing, slight burning, and ammonia fuming. With whatever coloring method you decide to go with, find out more about the type of wood that best agrees with the coloring method and the potential hazards linked to it.

Ease of working with

The hardwoods are a bit tougher to work with, and they also have a negative impact on sharp tools resulting in the constant need to sharpen such tools. If you use tools made out of carbide, you won't face any problems. On the other hand, softwoods are a beauty to work with as they pose no challenges when turning. However, they have some downsides, such as the size of wood that can be conveniently worked on and the final product most times are easily damaged due to their relatively soft nature.

To make your wood selection process easier, keep records of your past experiences and the project you worked on. You can go back to check the price, qualities, and how the wood responded to turning, the finish application, etc. With these invaluable details in hand, you won't have trouble picking a wood species for your project.

Preparing a log

You will most likely have witnessed a branch of a tree fall off or a whole tree uprooted due to the force of a great wind. Such logs can be cut and turned into a blank to be used for your turning projects. The part of the tree to be used for the creation of a blank is very important. The tree's limb has a large number of concentrated growth rings and knots, which are liable to undergo warping and cracking. This can put your wood turned project in jeopardy; to avoid wasting time and resources, make use of only the trunks.

Immediately you obtain the desired trunk, apply a wood sealer to the open ends to avoid them drying out. Avoid the use of paraffin because it can stain your wood and also cracks and breaks off. The use of a sealer is to avoid checking. Sometimes, you will come across an old fallen log of wood that has undergone checking due to one exposed end. In such situations, cut the checked end to reveal a fresh area and then apply the sealing agent quickly. The wood logs should be stored in an airy area and should not be cut into pieces until you are ready to make blanks out of them. This is to prevent too many surfaces from being exposed, resulting in checking. Also, do not remove the bark from the tree as this serves as a mechanism to prevent excessive water loss and, to a large extent, reduces the chances of checking to occur.

In cutting the wood into blanks, always cut it into pieces that are about 6 inches longer than the log's diameter. This is a preventive measure taken in case checking occurs; you have sealed and stored the blank, you can remove the affected area and still have your proposed wood size in mind. Set the log of wood down on a stable surface and secure it properly to avoid it slipping or rolling over. The cut should go in the grain direction as this is easier and prevents the dulling of the blade. There is less resistance from the fibers of the wood if the cut is not against the grain. Some woods need that the exposed areas be sealed, but the entire piece, especially when such species tend to dry out quickly. Properly identify the woods that will be coated and store all the blanks on an elevated platform.

The blanks should be regularly checked while in storage for the formation of molds, cracks, etc. If you observe cracks formation, cut off the affected parts immediately to avoid the whole log from being affected. The blanks should be stored in shaded cool areas, and there should be ample spaces between the logs to prevent damp and the growth of mold.

The log doesn't need to be cut lengthwise, especially when you have other plans, allowing you to turn a relatively large bowl from the log. This method is called the end-grain technique, and it is more complicated than the face-grain method. The face-grain is more preferred due to its resistance to cracking as against the end-grain types.

Chapter Five
Turning Green Wood Bowls

The transformation of green wood into a beautiful turned work of art is a process that every woodturner looks forwards to and will always cherish. No matter the woodturning project that you have envisaged, it will grow out of a piece of green log. You should know that the nature of wood is always changing; you must be able to tap into this unique nature of wood to make the best of it and not be blindsided by changes you never envisioned. Have an open mind and be ready to adapt to whatever the new piece of log presents to you as you turn some work of art every time you work at the lathe.

Dry and Wet

Bowl blanks can be generally divided into dried or wet/green bowl blanks. The majority of woodturners will most likely have been using the dried variety due to the lack of a drying mechanism for the logs. This can cost quite a log; thus, this section is dedicated to using readily available wet logs all around you for turning. Other than the associated costs of purchasing dried wood for turning, it should be noted that though greenwood is cheaper and easier to acquire, it has its downsides too.

Greenwoods are typically logs from a fresh tree or a piece of wood that has not undergone any form of seasoning. Greenwoods have a large amount of moisture, not regarding the time at which they were cut from the tree. Freshly cut logs will mostly have high contents of sap and other fluids, and woods that have been cut and allowed to sit for a while also have higher moisture contents than that of woods that have been seasoned and dried. The amount of moisture present in a piece of freshly cut log is also dependent on the time of the year when it was cut. Any wood, either freshly cut or not that still has moisture that can be removed is termed a greenwood.

On the other hand, dry wood is a piece of wood that has had all its moisture removed till there is no more moisture present in it. Dry wood majorly has the moisture removed through seasoning, allowing the log to sit for a long time in a favorable environment for drying or making use of a drying mechanism such as a kiln. If time is of the essence and you will rather have the wood dried faster, then the use of a kiln or a microwave oven is advised.

When talking about the moisture content in wood and the dryness, it should be noted that dry wood's moisture content is significantly lower than that of greenwood. Dry wood still has some form of moisture in it as it will always absorb and release moisture. This is a condition that is determined by the environment and the season. So have the mindset that dry wood is not a permanent state, assume it to be a form of material that lets out moisture and absorbs some more based on either favorable or unfavorable conditions. If the environment is humid, the supposedly dry wood will absorb a relatively high amount of moisture and become slightly "wet." If the atmosphere is dry and devoid of humidity, the wood will give out its stored water. This phenomenon can be observed in household furniture through constant movements of joints and other areas on the wood if no finishing is applied to limit this in and out movement of moisture.

So why are we so bothered about the moisture content of our logs? Moisture is responsible for the definite shape associated with wood, and if this is affected negatively or positively, the shape of the log will also undergo significant changes. This result in wood movement and this can be obvious or hidden from the human eyes. You can observe this in your wooden furniture undergoing expansion and contraction, giving rise to odd shapes, most especially around the piece's joints.

Cracking

In turning green wood, several potential downsides can make the whole experience a nightmare for any woodturner. However, cracking stands tall amongst them all, and it happens as a result of the drying process within the wood not evenly distributed. For example, when a part of a turned wood is thicker compared to other areas, there will be an uneven ability to take in and release moisture into the environment. When such a piece is allowed to undergo drying, there is a very high possibility of cracking. The uneven shape of the piece is not the only factor responsible for cracking, as the unique nature of the log also gives rise to a variation in the pressure rates in the different parts of the log. For example, in the middle part of the log, the core is highly susceptible to cracking. The other areas around it will always continually send and receive moisture from this region. Problems such as cracking are best solved by ensuring that they do not get to happen at all. In all your turning, make sure that all sides of the project are even in thickness, most especially with greenwood.

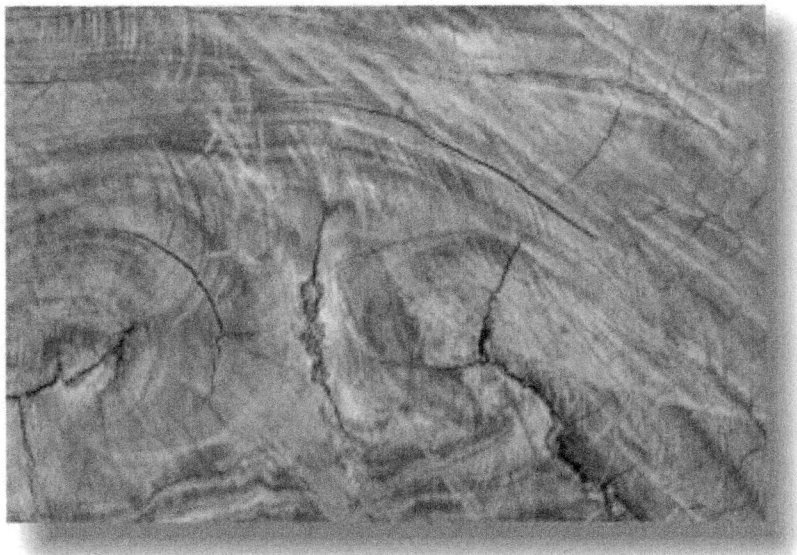

If it is to be included in the project, the pith, e.g., a bowl, is best if it is situated along the bowl's side. Do not allow the pith to be fixed on the rim. Though the position and inclusion of the bowl might not be that important, the fact is that you should try to maintain an even thickness for the bowl down the side and at the bottom.

As the green wood turned bowl dries, there will be obvious changes in the project's overall shape. Beginners most times will have the notion that the green turned bowl will maintain the perfect shape that it had after turning; they couldn't be more wrong. There will be distortions, warping, and other shape alterations as the drying process continue. Turning green wood is not ideal for making a project with exact measurements when it has finally "dried" out. Before you start any project making use of greenwood, be certain that you will be willing to embrace the outcome after it has dried out.

Important factors in turning greenwood bowls

Turning greenwood is a delightful experience that you won't want to come to an end anytime soon. It is easier than hard, dried wood with the turnings gently flowing down to the floor. Greenwood has different features that must be taken into consideration before you begin to work on it. When mounting your bowl, the mortise or the tenon must be of the correct size so that a firm hold is ensured on the bottom of the bowl. To secure the faceplate, regular screws might not be the best option; it will be best to use long screws to offer a better hold on the wet wood. With dry wood, you can take your time in turning the blank; that is, you can turn the outside and wait for a few days before continuing with the inner part of the bowl. However, with greenwood, once you begin with the turning, you have to finish the process at a go. This is because intermittent turning will produce unwanted results such as checks and cracks before you get to finish turning the blank. With wet wood, sanding can also be done though there are a few folks who assume it is impossible. Sanding wet wood can be different as the sanding paper will get affected, and the amount of slurry produced will make it hard to get the sanding done effectively. There are ways around these little obstacles by using mesh sanding disks that work more effectively than the regular sanding paper. You can also wait for about 20 – 30 minutes to allow some of the moisture to dry out before you begin to sand.

You should carry out a test run on the greenwood that you intend to turn. If you have some pieces of wet wood around you of a certain species, turn three bowls of different wall thicknesses and allow them to dry. After a few days, observe them and check if there are any noticeable changes such as cracks, deformation, warping or movements. When this same test is performed on a different tree species, you will most likely get a different set of results.

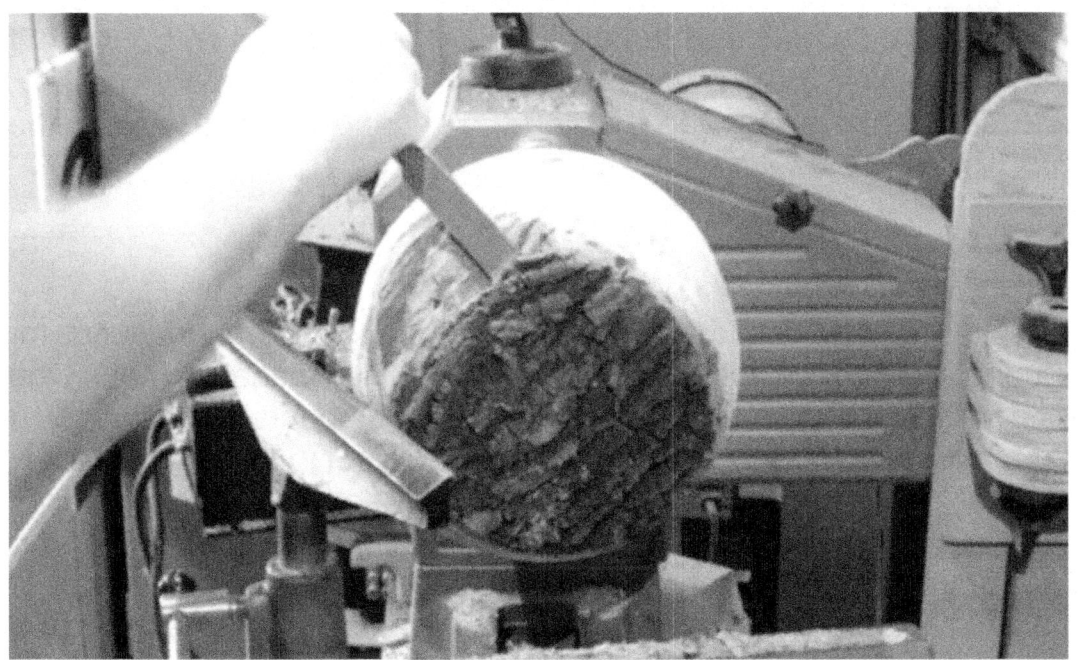

Twice Turned

Greenwood can be turned twice by carrying out an initial turning of the wood to get a rough bowl shape and allowing it to dry out for a few days. Due to the changes that will occur as the wood undergoes drying, take out a measured amount of wood and create a uniform wall all around the bowl to prevent warping, cracking, etc. The second turning carried out will then aim to get the fine and desired design you want from the process due to the considerable loss of moisture.

It is pertinent that you get the width of the wall correctly during the first turning. Ideally, if the bowl's diameter is 12 inches, the wall should be 1.2 inches wide. The reason for having a wall that is 10% the size of the diameter of the bowl is that when drying occurs, the pith elongates, and the bowl deforms. The perfect circular shape that you had initially will be gradually changed into something oval. With the size of the wall that you have, there will be sufficient wood for you to work on during the second turning to get a rounded bowl. It also makes sense that the walls are of that dimension because if they are thicker, it will require an extended time for it to dry properly, and also, if the wall is too thin, on the second turning, there is the probability that it will be damaged.

Why Greenwood?

Despite all the "issues" surrounding the use of greenwood for turning, you should be aware of the immense benefits that come with its use. For example, the massive amounts of wood dust generated when dry wood is used is not a factor. The air is relatively cleaner and safer to breathe. The wood's soft nature also makes your lathe tools last longer as they don't dull it, and the moisture acts as a cooling agent when turning. Have you considered the cost of purchasing dry wood? With greenwood, it is most time free and abundant all over the environment. Another beautiful aspect of greenwood is the variety and serendipity; where you obtain a piece for another project is a game of chance. You won't likely obtain a piece of greenwood from the same place in a long time. This diverse means of obtaining your wood confers on the piece a sense of uniqueness that you won't get from dry wood.

Using greenwood for your turnings gets you actively involved in all the steps, from obtaining the wood to finishing the turned wooden piece. This is lacking with the dry wood as you come in halfway and would have lost the opportunity to connect with your blank.

Wood that would have had another fate is converted to a piece of art that would last for a long time and bring countless people joy.

Chapter Six

Sharpening Lathe Tools

It is a monumental roadblock trying to get sharpened tools to employ for woodturning sessions for most beginners. Without the proper knowledge, even folks with some form of experience are guilty of not paying attention to the role that sharp tools play and the relatively simple steps involved in sharpening existing tools. If you are not properly grounded in the basics of sharpening your tools, woodturning will most likely be a nightmare for even the most persevering individual. With an adequately sharpened tool, you will not be forced to endure heartbreak after heartbreak. Every woodturning project will be a joy to behold as there will be almost no problem making that almost perfect bowl.

For tool sharpening, you need to have some tools at your disposal. Listed below are the most important.

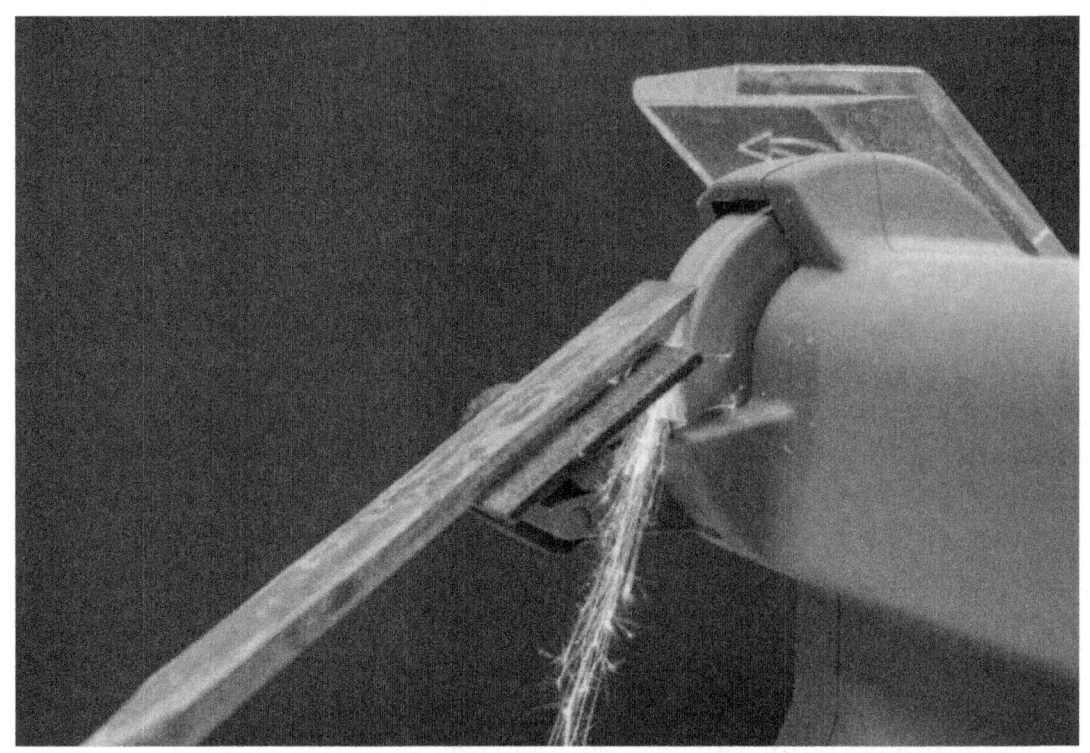

The Grinder

Without the grinder, there is not going to be any sharpening happening anytime soon. Grinders come in two main sizes; 8-inch and 6-inch grinders, which will sharpen or reshape your tools without hassles. The grinder is typically mounted on a workbench or any other secure and stable surface that will make the sharpening process easy. When purchasing a grinder, go for one that has at least 3000 rpm that can be used for both domestic and commercial applications. Such grinders have relatively low decibel ratings and do not vibrate as others, not in the category.

Other implements needed are;
Wheel dresser
Eye protection
Dry cloth
Sharpening jigs

Rubber gloves
Lathe tools
Bucket
Water

Using a Grinder to Sharpen Woodturning Tools

Preparations

Before you begin to sharpen your lathe tools, you must check that all the appropriate personal protective wears are available. Put on the rubber gloves, eye goggles, respirator and ensure that the grinder is properly fixed to the work surface before you turn it on. During the sharpening, the grinder should not be too far from you to prevent the tool from getting stuck between the grinder and the sharpening platform.

Just like with other implements in your workshop, the grinder must be looked after regularly and, if possible, after every sharpening. When used, there is always an accumulation of tiny metallic slivers that can reduce its operational capabilities. To get this under check, the grinder dressing is advised with the aid of a diamond sharpening tool, which should be applied to the extremities of the wheel.

Grinding Angles

The lathe tools all have significant differences in the cutting angles. Based on this, sharpening angles for the lathe tools will not be the same. For example, the cutting angle for the skew chisel is different from that of the gouge. Some tools have a very shallow sharpening angle, which means that a great deal of skill is needed for the process without damaging the tool. If you are not conversant with the sharpening of lathe tools, you should start with sharp-angled lathe tools before moving on to those with higher angles of inclination, e.g., start with 65° before moving to a tool with a lesser angle (55°).

Listed below are the grinding angles of the common lathe tools
- Bowl gouge (50° – 60°)
- Flat parting tool (45°)
- Roughing gouge (35° – 45°)

- Spindle gouge (35° – 45°)
- Diamond parting tool (45°)

The Contact

With you getting comfortable and knowledgeable about the angles that you should grind at, there needs to be an appropriate contact between the tool and the grinder for the right angle of sharpening to be produced. The way to go is to ensure that the lathe tool is sitting conveniently on its rest before any workings are carried out. Continue with this till the wheel and tool are touching each other. The contact should be minimal between the tool, and the wheel should be minimal at the correct angle. If the tool's pressure is too hard against the grinder, there is the possibility that there will be the production of a lot of vibrations, which might be too much for you to handle; thus, the tool will likely be freed from your hand.

The First Stage

With the tool now in position next to the grinder, gently push it forward at the correct angle until it contacts the grinder. The duration should not exceed about 10 to 12 seconds, and there will be the production of a high screeching sound and sparks flying if you got the duration and angle of contact correct. Move-in a sideways fashion while you closely observe how the sparks are produced; if you are getting it, you will see the sparks along with the tool and grinder's outer portion.

The Second Stage

Carry out the above process a few times, not exceeding the stated number of seconds. Check if the tool is sharp enough for you, and immerse it into a container filled with water. The grinder and the tool will generate a massive amount of heat during the process, so be careful not to touch any of the implements with your bare hands and ensure that you are properly kitted. With the tool's temperature sufficiently reduced, use a piece of cloth to remove all the moisture and make sure that it is properly dried before grinding again. Begin the sharpening process with the other side. The grinding should be equally done for both sides of the tool to prevent any deficiencies that will lead to damage and the tool's inability to perform its functions.

If you have had your lathe machine for a few days and you have been turning on it, you will understand the need to sharpen your wood as it will have been dulled slightly with the constant turning of wood at high speeds.

Chapter Seven

Techniques

Bowl Blanks from Logs

The preparation of bowl blanks from fresh logs is a step in the woodturning process that gives as much pleasure as holding the final piece in your hands. Logs are everywhere you look, easy to come by, and you honestly have no idea what the outcome will be like for every project due to the personality of each log piece. The steps involved in getting your blanks require that you know how to handle a bandsaw, as it is the basic tool used for this preparation. The production of blanks starts with determining which parts of the tree will give you well-turned outcomes. Different parts of the tree have unique grain arrangements, so you need to be familiar with applying it to your wood piece. Using a band saw, which is essential for the blank's preparation, needs to factor in the blade type to be used. If an inappropriate blade type is used, there will be issues both for the bowl blank you are working on and the machine itself. It also saves you a lot of time to have as many blanks as possible.

Chatter

The lathe can comfortably turn materials that are within its capacity to handle. However, turning of spindles tend to create a small problem on getting to a certain stage. When you begin to turn the spindle, it will proceed smoothly until a sudden vibration of the lathe begins causing the previously smooth surface to become slightly rough and disfigured. This phenomenon is known as lathe chatter. This is a nightmare for any woodworker turning a spindle. Even when you try to solve all the suspected issues pointing to the chatter, you still find yourself tortured by the problem.

To solve this seemingly elusive problem, you need to be able to identify its cause. Chatter is produced in the middle part of the spindle because it does not have firm support compared to the ends being held in place by the tailstock and headstock. To get this problem under control, you will have to get some form of support mechanism in place at the center of the work. You can get it done by;

 Using your hand to support the mid part of the spindle while turning gently. You, however, must put all safety measures in place before doing this. A pair of gloves and your goggles is a must.

 The other method requires that you purchase a steady rest. This apparatus distributes a uniform pressure along the length of the spindle.

Spindle Turning Foundation

Before putting on the machine, check to ensure that it is at the correct speed setting for the project at hand. For a turning project, there are three distinct stages, roughing, shaping, and sanding. Any one of these stages has a speed limit that works best for it.

First, you have to mount the spindle blank and rough it; this involves taking out all the angled corners to produce a cylindrical wooden piece. At this point, the speed level is relatively slow, and the tool of choice can be a roughing gouge or a spindle gouge. Using the roughing gouge, with the tool pointing blade downwards, one hand firmly holding onto the handle and the other hand resting on the chisel, carefully place your pointing finger next to the tool rest. Adjust the tool rest close to the spindle without contact been made by the two. Switch on the machine and carefully move the gouge onto the blank. Work down the blank's length, gently taking out all the sharp edges to make the whole blank circular rather than rectangular. To confirm if the roughing is going on as planned, switch off the machine, and use a visual cue to check. You can also leave the lathe on and place the backside of the gouge against the blank; if there is an uneven movement, that is an indication that the material is not fully rounded.

With the roughing done, move onto shaping of the spindle blank. Confirm that all the angles have been removed before you proceed with this step. The speed of the lathe can also be slightly increased for the creation of contours. Here, the skew is the focus tool, and you will need to put in some practice hours to master it fully. The flat side of the skew should be blade should work on the valleys. Avoid getting the sharp areas of the blade into the surface of the spindle.

In shaping a spindle, there are three main parameters to be considered, which are; coves, beads, and aiming for a predetermined diameter. The coves are concave in shape, while the beads have a convex appearance. These two additions are often added to spindles as aesthetics and beautifying features. When you want a certain diameter met, it is most often because the spindle's ends are to be inserted into a piece of furniture, e.g., the legs of a chair or rails.

To begin with, indicate the areas of interest on the cylindrical spindle blank with a pencil. To create coves, the spindle gouge is used, and the process is a breeze. Carefully push the spindle gouge into the wood's surface in the area you have designated for the coves. Ensure that you start the process from the topmost part and move gently downwards. A wide gouge will not produce deep and narrow coves; this is the narrow spindle gouge's specialty area. You can make use of a wide variety of spindle gouges to move the shapes to the spindle.

To produce beads, place the skew's sharp edge on the drawn line and the other cutting part focused on the portion where the bead is to be formed. Gently move the sharp part of the skew into the blank and simultaneously turn the other part of the cutting edge to the bead parts. Turn around the chisel and carry out the same process in the opposite area.

The necessary tools are the calipers and the parting tool to get the size of the diameter that you want. Adjust the caliper to the desired diameter settings and then begin to make an ever-increasing groove on the surface for the spindle while at the same time regularly checking the size with the calipers. While making the groove, make sure that it is the same size all around the spindle. After a groove has been constructed, brush out the sawdust to get the correct caliper readings.

While working on the spindle diameter, there will be a need to make constant alterations to the tool rest as it should not contact the spindle but be near it. With the reduction in the diameter of the spindle, the tool rest will have to be adjusted to keep the distance between it and the spindle constant. You also adjust the tool's height so that it is at a central position on the spindle. This prevents the constant need for you to keep making changes.

Oval Turning

Oval turning can be successfully performed on the lathe through the use of multi-axis turning. This technique is carried out by shifting the action or live center to two or more areas on the spindle to form exotic rounded shapes. Moving from creating the more comfortable rounded spindle to the oval can be a bit tough when you are starting out, but all you need is to understand a few techniques, and you will be on your way to turning smooth ovals in no time. Follow the steps listed below;

- Indicate the locations where you want to work and use a suitable marking tool to make the points by forming a slight groove or indentation at the various points. All this will be determined by the type of oval shape you want to create.
- Move the live center to the point of interest and beginning to turn until a predetermined size is achieved. Then proceed to the other points and carry out the same procedure all over.
- Now, move to the middle point to finish the process. This will cut down on the total size of the oval. The life center can be moved back to the offset points if there is a need to adjust the oval's shape.
- When the desired oval shape has been achieved, go from one offset point to the other, sanding it and making sure that the connections from one point to the other is seamless and smooth.

The Turning of a Tenon on a 4-Jaw Chuck

The inclusion of a 4-jaw chuck ups the ability to turn larger blanks and make the process relatively easy. With the proper technique, the 4-jaw chuck should ideally have a tenon placed in the chucks to allow for a thorough securing of the bowl blank and turning at speeds that will ensure that the bowl comes out looking nice while all safety protocols are observed. Follow the steps listed below;

- ➢ Using a screw chuck, mount the bowl blank.
- ➢ Carry out a turning of the blank to makes sure that it is circular to ensure that it is well centered and won't go off balance when the proper turning begins.
- ➢ Form a tenon that is the right size for the 4-jaw chuck.
- ➢ Place the tenon into the chuck and check that the lower end of the bowl blank is not on the tenon; it should be on the 4-jaw chucks. This will provide stability when the lathe starts to turn.

Chapter Eight
Copy turning

The process of copy turning is done on special lathes, which control the cutting tool in some manner to generate identical items.

There is a template that the copy lathe uses to guide the cutter. This will enable the creation of good quality components for small expense in patterns and setting up. In this case, sanding is often done by hand.

When the lathes are full, they may employ profile tools or rotary tooling to get the desired outline. The lathes are equally able to produce work quickly with a quality finish. However, these machines often depend on machine sanding, which might not always retain fine detail. Therefore, they need special tooling and considerable set up for every job.

Often, those who are inexperienced in copy turning might find it intimidating. But it is not. It only takes consistent practice with two or more pieces to achieve the needed expertise.

Copy turning attachment

The attachment for your lathe is usually one option, but having many items to perform the task will be worthwhile. You must ensure that the attachment is paid for, set up, and taken down. However, they may get in the way when they are not used. It may not even save time. Saving yourself time and money is crucial when you engage in hand turning. Once you become consistent with the practice, you will soon be good at making duplicates in no-time—practice and consistency are the keys to building your skills and confidence. Hence, you should be passionate about turning when you take up woodturning.

The set of turnings you make needs to be similar to each other and the original pattern, even though it hardly happens. There are usually slight variations, which is quite okay because they go a long way to indicate that your items are handmade. This variation is evident in antique furniture, where they're slight variations in the spindles, even though that shouldn't be an excuse for sloppiness. In general, the closer together the two items are placed, the more closely they should lookalike.

Critical dimensions
The overall length, the maximum and minimum diameters, the diameter of any tenon or fitting, and the position of beads or other prominent features are often the most dimensions of copying a spindle. The exact size of beads, fillets, and coves is critical. Hence you need to mark out, measure, and turn with care to achieve an even job.

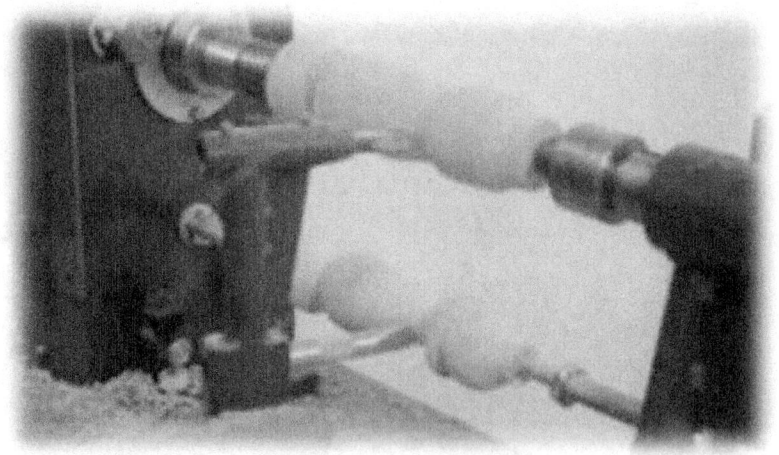

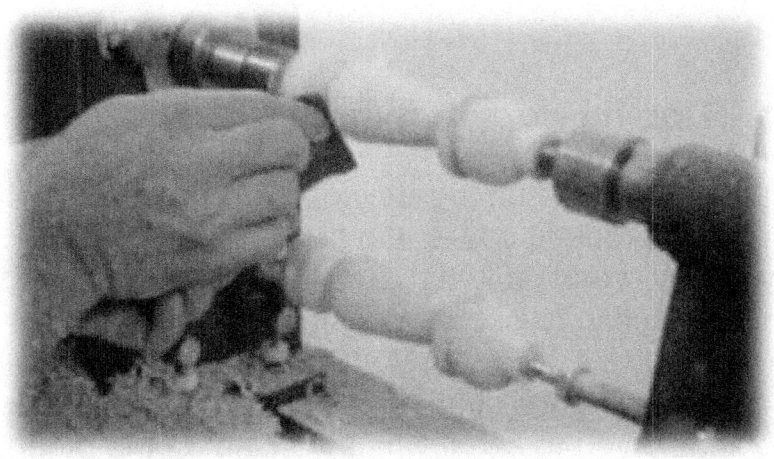

Tips for copy turning

- Don't attempt copy turning (except for practice) until you're able to produce coves and beads reliably.
- Once you can reasonably turn, make one complete item to your satisfaction to show that you're capable of doing the job.
- Make a holder for the item and position it behind the lathe to enable you to see it when working on the others.
- Break the task down into various steps and put the items through every stage when working on them before going to the next item. By doing this, you can use the practice gained from the first, and you can also see that each one is within tolerance limits as you proceed.
- Start with some spares to give room for any rejects that might occur.
- Taking each step gradually, the turning process becomes a breeze working with, errors will become far in between,

and you will develop confidence and work swiftly at every stage.
- Have a motley collection of scrap wood to work with. This makes for easier copying if making the blanks identical is what you're starting with.
- Have a stack of cylinders of the same size, but make them a bit more than the finished piece's maximum diameter to allow sanding.

Marking Out

The templates used in woodturning are typically designed by indicating important points from the sample directly to the material to be used. This is then placed onto the blanks and drawn out with the appropriate types of pencils. The pertinent points vary in number based on how accurate the turning process will be for the copies to be made. The bead's centerline for individual beads can be clearly marked, the total length of the item been worked on, and also the position where the tenon will occupy. To make the turning easier, you can omit the beads' width as having too many markings on the blank can be a complicated process rather than simplifying the turning process. For jobs that will be repeated at a future date, it is best that you properly attach the necessary information to the template that will enable you to replicate it when needed.

Tool Preparation

- It goes without saying that all tools for the process must be properly sharpened and carry out all the needed measurements with calipers. When using the calipers to measure out the diameters, leave a bit of room for potential errors and the obvious sanding that will later have to be carried out.
- If a softwood is being worked on, there is the likelihood that the calipers might cause undesirable markings on it.

So do avoid using it at the top of the bead.
- Make use of the appropriate type of calipers for the bead sizes you have in mind. With a bit of experience under your belt, you will be able to visually gauge the size of the diameter needed.
- A parting tool can be employed alongside the calipers to get the desired diameters.
- The diameters determined part on both sides of the block for the beads on the lines you have marked out.
- The parting cuts should fully connect the beads and put allowances for the skew or gouge. There are situations in which there will be no allowances for partings if there are to be beads lying next to each other. In this case, create a V cut with a skew or any other equipment.

Shape Turning

When you are copy turning, there is a sequence that should be followed to get the end product you want; beads, coves, and finally fillets. Ensure that the beads and coves are properly shaped, and the fillets all have uniform widths to ensure that all the measurements taken are produced. When you are through with the production of the set, properly examine them, and remove the ones with defects. All you need to do is turn two or three of the blanks, indicate the positions of the features such as the beads, coves, curves, etc., to fit into the tenons.

Chapter Nine
Finishing
Sanding

To get that smooth and impeccable finish on your turned wood, you should try to sand it while it is still mounted on the lathe. Sanding with the lathe is relatively easy; the tool rest is taken off, and sandpaper of the desired grit is held firmly in place against the turned wood, and the lathe is then activated. The speed at which the sanding is carried out should be far lesser than the turning speed as an increased speed will produce more heat and could ignite the work and the paper. The sandpaper should not be held at the top side of the piece as this will direct the wood dust towards you. Hold the paper under the piece below the work while continuously moving it to prevent too much heat from being generated before sanding with sandpaper, first aim to smoothen the wood as much as you can with the aid of a skew chisel.

You can take the sanding of your projects to be a hassle that must be endured if you can embrace and enjoy every minute of it to produce unique wood turned objects. A well-finished project will always stand out and turn heads in whichever room it sits. Ideally, sanding should not be an option; it should be a must. Sandpaper comes in different grits; the smaller the grit size, the coarser the paper. For example, a paper with grit size of, let's say, 320 is finer when compared to one with a grit size of 150.

Like with any woodworking project that needs to undergo sanding, you begin with removing ugly gouges and markings to create some form of smoothness before proceeding. This first stage of sanding will accentuate the features of that particular project. You should move up gradually on the grit scale with sanding and not jump from 50 to 180. Rather you can move from sanding with 50 to 8o to 120. There should be a gradual increment in the changing of the paper used. The typical grit sizes of paper are; 50, 80, 120, 150, 180, 220, 320, 400, 600 and 800. Jumping from a smaller grit size and skipping more than one grit size won't smoothen out the markings left behind by the last paper used. This will make it almost impossible to get rid of the marks made by the last paper used.

After sanding, always clean the turned wood with a clean rag as there are always dust and grit left on the turned wood after sanding. The presence of dirt and grits on the surface of the work will produce unwanted markings when you move on to the next size of sandpaper, and it will slow down your progress, which you don't want.

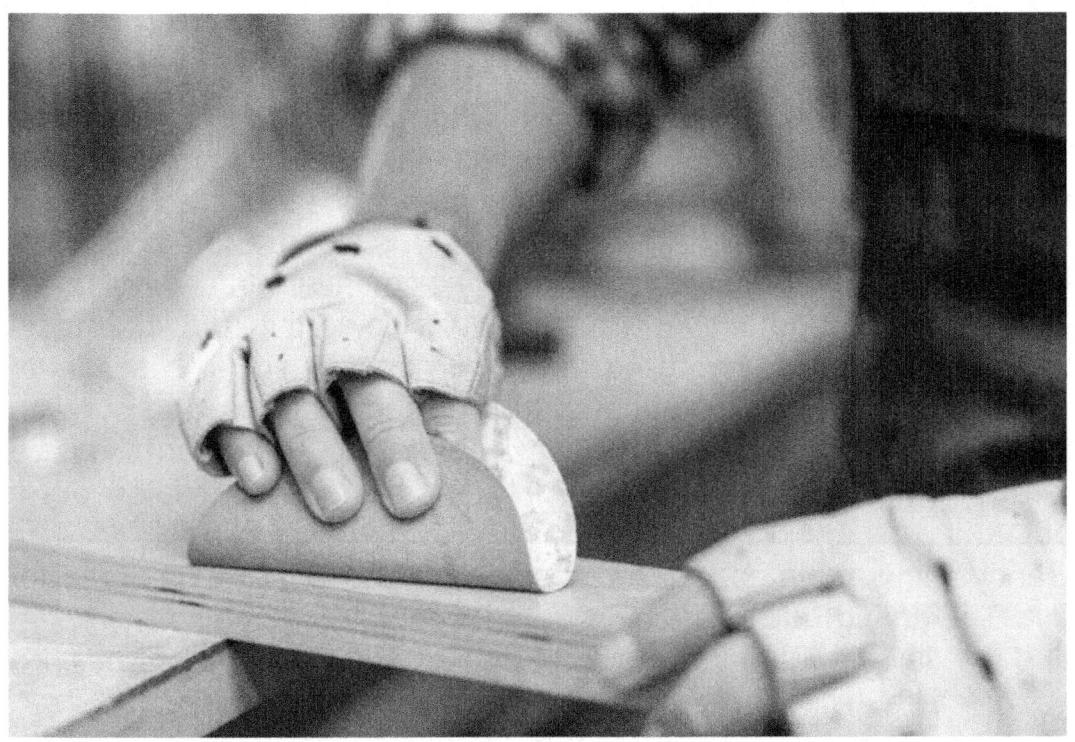

NOTE

Sanding making use of the lathe generates a large amount of waste in sawdust and grit. You can reduce the amount of dust dispersed into the air by applying some form of moisture to the wood's surface. In all, always protect yourself with a respirator or dust mask.

Other than the sanding paper, other materials are used for the finishing process. They include and are not limited to;

Polishing papers and cloths

The term used varies among users, but the papers are used to apply oils and polish, while the cloth is used for the application of waxes and sanding sealer. In using a paper cloth, be aware that some of such cloths have some abrasive properties.

With experience and some searching, you will get a cloth that is the perfect fit for your projects. It is pertinent to note that on no account should you ever make use of the cloth or paper wrapped around your fingers while applying finishes.

The method I use in making my wood turned projects flawless time after time follows this simple and easy to follow guidelines.

I start with the sanding of the exterior part of the project, which I have discussed earlier. After the sanding is done and the bowl or object still mounted, quickly apply a sufficient layer of sanding sealer to the surface to get it evenly moist. While doing this, the lathe must be off. Move on to getting rid of the surplus sealer using a mutton cloth piece, allow it dry properly, turn on the machine and burnish. When the burnishing is done, use a Nyweb to smoothen it out by removing the uneven surface. Apply another coat of sealer, dry it out, and cut it again.

Gently apply a thin coat of paste wax and give it a few hours to dry out. The drying rate is affected by environmental conditions; on hot and dry days, it will dry faster than on wet and cold days. Switch on the machine, pick a new piece of clean cloth, and burnish it.

The same procedure used for the exterior of the bowl can also be applied to the interior. However, the sanding paper's size should be larger than that used for the exterior sanding as it makes the process faster.

Oil application

The application of oil is a bit time consuming and requires your undivided attention to give the wood solidity and finesse. The use of oil during the sanding of the turned project has additional benefits like reducing the amount of sawdust produced and giving the wood a pleasing warm glow. After the normal sanding, you can then move onto the finishing with the oil. Protect the lower part of the lathe with suitable coverings to prevent oil from dropping and spilling on it. Follow the guidelines listed below to apply oil to your wood turned project;

- Generously apply oil to the wood using a brush and allow it to sit for 15 to 20 minutes. This will allow the excess oil to drip away and give it time to penetrate the wood's fibers.
- Apply some more oil and use sandpaper of grit size 320 on the bowl with the lathe operating minimally. Gently

- allow the sandpaper to make contact with the bowl.
- Don't stop the sanding until you observe the formation of a semi-solid mass accumulating on the wood. Sand for a few more minutes.
- Stop the machine and thoroughly clean the bowl; switch on the machine again and burnish with paper.
- Unmount the bowl and set it down in a clean environment for a day.
- After this, apply a new coat of oil, allow it to sit for about an hour before wiping it. Repeat this process three to four times before you polish it with wax.

Friction Polishing

This process is often misconstrued, and for those without adequate knowledge on how it works, the application and use is often done wrongly. Friction polish is not ideal for large projects such as bowls but is a good fit with bottle stoppers and cord pulls. To apply friction polish, begin with sanding the piece, apply the sealer with a small brush, use a mutton cloth to remove the excess sealer, and burnish it simultaneously. The lathe can be used for this. Cut the excess sealer with a Nyweb. Use a small brush to apply the friction polish and rub away the excess and burnish at the same time with a well-folded piece of paper.

Several products can be used for specific woodturning projects. Some of these products can be made at home if you have the right recipe and implements to put them together safely. This can get you involved personally in every step of the wood turned project and save you some bucks. Whether you are purchasing the finished products from a store or making your product, always read the directions on the ingredients' pack as they most times contain toxic and often flammable compounds if incorrectly handled. Find below the commonly used finishing materials;

- Wax

- Oil-based materials
- Sealers
- Lacquer
- Shellac

These materials come in various brands and combinations to suit the varying needs of woodworkers. Before purchasing or using any finish on your product, carry out a test by applying it on a scrap piece of wood to confirm that it agrees with what you have in mind. Read the packaging of the products; this is very important.

Chapter Ten
Projects
Bowls

Supplies
Dividers
Scraper (round nose and curved)
Four-jaws chuck
Finish
Bowl gouge
Faceplate
Double-ended calipers
Sanding pads
Lathe
Wood

Directions
- ❖ Load and mount the chosen faceplate onto the middle part of the blank and hold it firmly in place with the aid of the appropriate screws.
- ❖ To the headstock, link and firmly fix the faceplate while at the same time securing the blank with the tailstock.
- ❖ Gently push the hand brake to check that bowl blank doesn't come in contact with the tool rest. The bowl blank should also be properly balanced by checking it from the tailstock and moving front to the headstock.
- ❖ After you must have carried out the step above, level up the blank through a process called "trueing up" and make use of a four-jawed chuck to form a spigot.
- ❖ The shaping of the bowl should begin from the outer layers of the bowl blank, and the cutting motion should be from the rear to the foremost part in a single move to prevent the formation of a ridged appearance.

- Bring the divider into play to determine the width of the four-jawed-chuck and at the same time, look out that the right leg of the divider doesn't at any point touch the bowl been turned.
- Reduce the width of the spigot for it to be comfortably accommodated by the chuck.
- With the bowl's rough shape, a power sander can then be used to smoothen it up and remove unwanted markings.
- Now set the bowl into the chuck.
- The bevel of the bowl gouge and the surface of the bowl must lay parallel to each other and determine how thick you want the bowl's wall to be. Determine and fix the gouge before switching on the machine.
- Repeat the passes from the start of the cut to the finish to produce an even cut on the inner part of the bowl with the aid of the bevel.
- Intermittently check if your desired wall thickness has been achieved.
- How deep the bowl is can be checked with the aid of a ruler by placing a flat edge on the surface of the bowl blank.
- A nose scraper is used to take out the nub at the rear of the bowl after you are satisfied with how deep it is. The bottom of the bowl should be flat.
- Move on to power sanding the bowl's inner part with a sander like the Abralon pad.
- Remove the spigot from the bottom of the bowl.
- You can then personalize your work through the addition of some fancy designs on the bottom and side of the bowl.
- If the bowl is to be used for serving food, the proper type of coating to be applied is the salad bowl finish.
- After the application of the finish and the bowl has been allowed to dry properly, make use of a sanding pad to sand the bowl once again before the application of the final layer of coating.

Fancy String Pulls

Supplies
Lathe
Wood scraps
Strings

Directions
- ❖ Mount the scrap wood to the lathe and round it to get rid of the rough edges. With the chuck firmly grasping the blank, the tailstock can be released to permit the lower part of the project's squaring.
- ❖ With the piece still mounted, drill a hole with the tiniest bit you can find into the blank. The hole goes from one end and comes out from the other end of the piece. With this done, you will now drill a second hole that goes in for about one-quarter of the length of the piece from the top. This second

hole is for housing the knot produced from the string and to stop the string from coming out all together.
- ❖ Move on to shaping the piece into any design pattern that you want.
- ❖ After the shaping is done, sand it properly, apply some coating, and wax it thoroughly.
- ❖ Insert the string into the hole previously drilled and then tie a double knot at the lower end of the string; pull the string up so that the knot is nestled in the hole.
- ❖ Your pull string is ready to be installed and used!

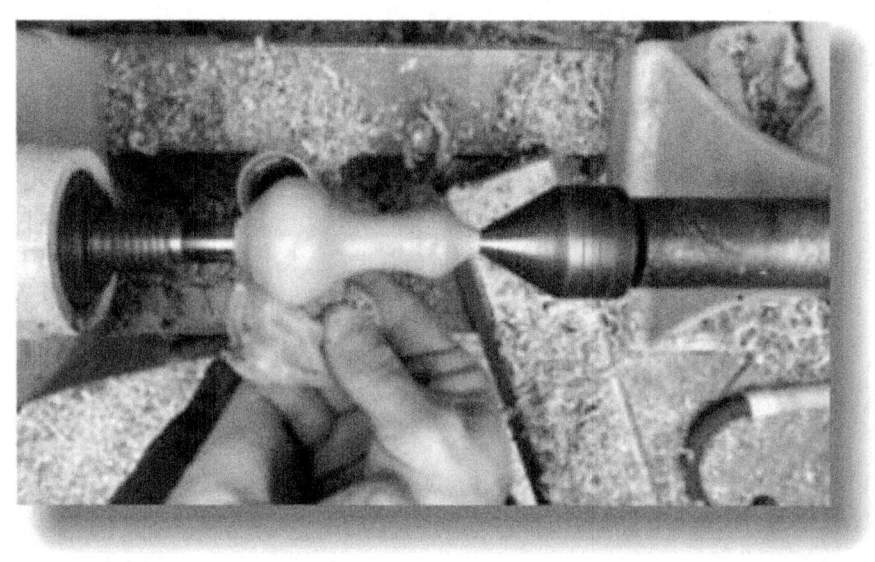

Weed Pots

Directions
- Mount the blank to the lathe.
- The size of the blank varies, and it depends on individual preferences.
- Form a tenon from two flats that are parallel to each other. The tenon will serve as a point of attachment for the chuck.
- With the tenon created, the spur can then be fixed to the chuck and then fix the tailstock to the piece firmly.
- Rough up the piece with a bowl gouge, release the tailstock, and set up the tool rest on the upper side of the weed pot to enable you to smoothen it out.
- Put back the tailstock and sand the exterior with a power sander.
- Mount a Jacob chuck onto the tailstock and drill bit and drill a hole to your requirements.
- Employ the round nose scraper to form the upper part of the pot to produce a concave shape, sand it and apply a coating of your choice.
- Allow the finish to dry before you part it off and carry out some waxing.

Wood Bangles

Supplies
A wood scrap disc of the desired diameter

Directions
- ❖ Rough turn the blank and flatten it.
- ❖ Use a sharp parting tool to create a hollow in the center of the disc. Map out the area to be cut inside the wood,

construct relief cuts, and cut about three quarters into the area marked out with the aid of the parting tool.
- ❖ With the depth reached, unmount the blank from the lathe, turn it over to the other side, place the jaws into it and screw it tightly into place.
- ❖ Draw out the radius with the parting tool and complete the cut.
- ❖ Carry out the power sanding of the inner area of the bangle and then proceed to sand the external part before you part the bracelet.
- ❖ With the sharp parting tool, designate the area, which will be the width of the bangle, while at the same time being mindful of the jaws so that there is no contact.
- ❖ After the parting is completed, sand the bangle manually, followed by buffing and finally waxing.

Pen

Supplies
Wood
Lathe
Pen kit
Sandpaper
Skew
Drill press
clamp
CA glue
Paper towels
Mandrel

Directions
- Cut the blank to enable it to fit the tubes.
- Drill holes in the blank with the aid of a hand drill or the lathe. The hole is to be square in shape and not round.
- Gently power sand the blank, spread a generous amount of glue onto the tube, and insert it into the blank. Push in and pull out the tube while at the same time twisting it to ensure that the glue covers all areas within the blank.
- Now, move on to squaring the blank and make sure you don't drill to the very end to prevent the tube from showing.
- Mount the blank on the bushings and the mandrel. The bushings will aid you in determining the level to which the turning of the wood will go. Employ the use of a chisel or gouge for the skew.
- Reduce the lathe and sand's speed with a grit of 220, then gradually move until the blank is smooth before you can then apply some boiled linseed oil with the aid of a paper towel.
- The finish application is done with glue, which should be smooth. Apply the glue with the paper towel to the lower part of the pen; this should be done quickly, and remove the paper towel to prevent it from sticking. A couple of coats will do just fine.

- ❖ Micromesh sand the pen with sandpaper ranging from about 1,400 to 11,000 grit.
- ❖ Beal buff and finally finish the pen with it still on the mandrel and lathe.
- ❖ Remove the pen from the mandrel and insert the transmission from the upper end, followed by the ink refill. This should be followed by fixing the clip on top of the pen and the spacer in between.

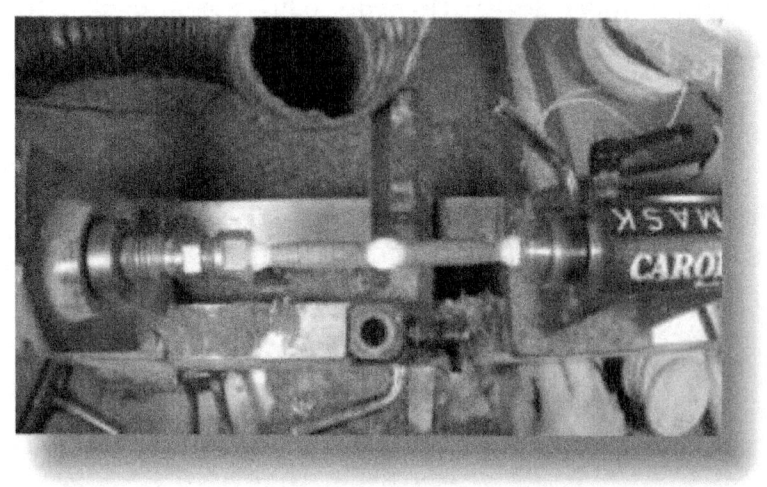

Wooden Mug

Supplies
Travel mug insert
4*4*10 piece of wood
Epoxy
Lathe

Directions
- ❖ Indicate the center of the project on the two ends of the blank for appropriate chucking on the machine.
- ❖ Rough the blank into a cylindrical shape.

- Create a tenon at one of the ends to enable the four jaw chuck to firmly hold onto the project.
- Make use of a Forstner bit to drill holes in the cylindrical blank. To be as accurate as possible, take measurements of the top, middle, and bottom parts of the mug insert, which will guide the drilled size. You can make use of a bowl gouge to produce the space.
- Work on the top of the blank where the mug insert fits in. Gently remove excess material to allow the insert to have a firm grip over this area. With the fitting achieved, mark that area so that you don't remove any more wood from there.
- Reduce the lathe's speed and sand it in reverse, gradually increasing the size of the grit.
- Part the mug from the stock with a parting tool.
- Apply a generous amount of the epoxy to the insert and then push it into the hollowed-out wooden project.
- Make use of the best method available to you to smoothen and flatten out the bottom of the mug.
- With the mug mounted, apply a food-grade oil finish with a paper towel.
- You are done!

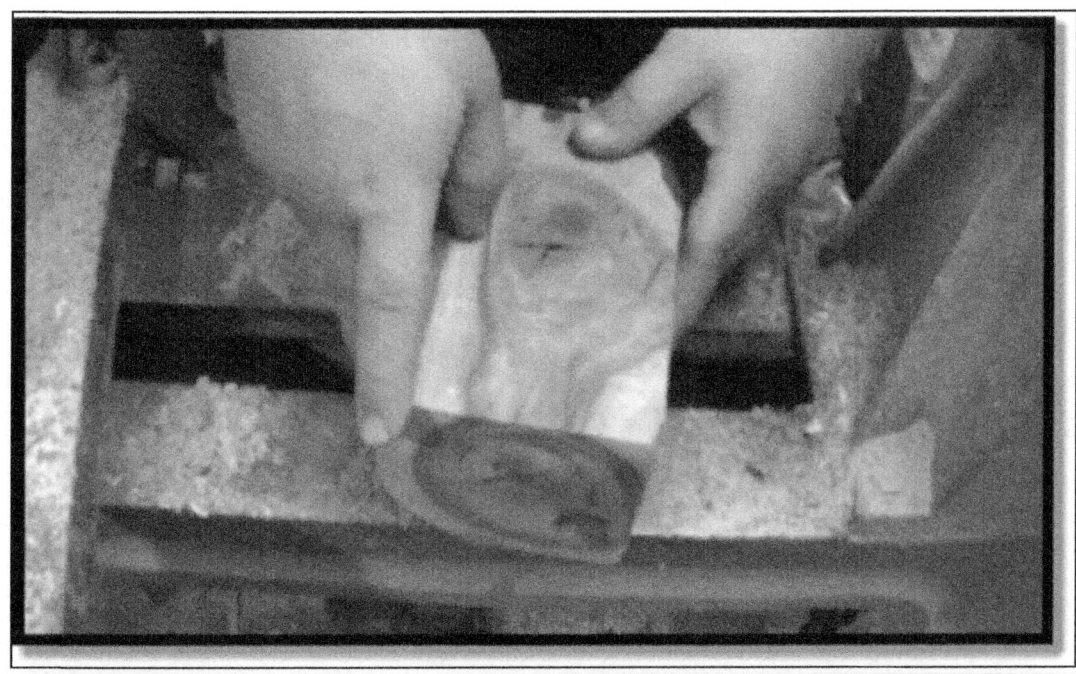
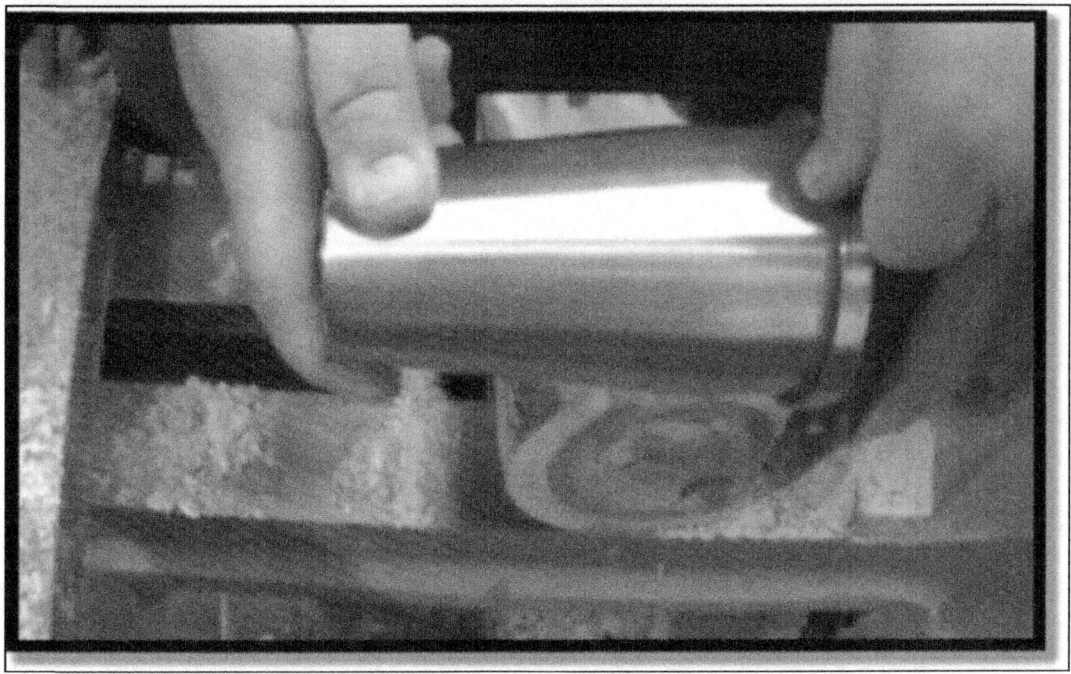

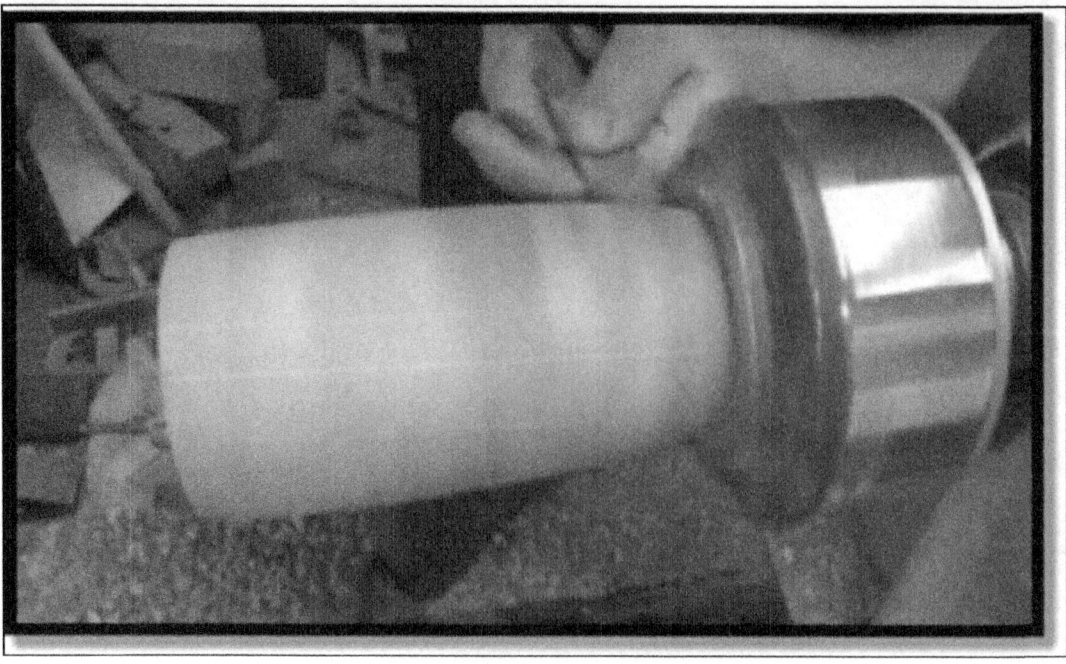

Printed in Great Britain
by Amazon